A Ch

I have endeavoured in this Ghostly little book, to raise the Ghost of an Idea, which shall not put my readers out of humour with themselves, with each other, with the season, or with me. May it haunt their houses pleasantly . . .

Charles Dickens, December 1843

Charles Dickens' *A Christmas Carol*, published in 1843, is one of the best-loved stories to be set at this time of year. The story has been adapted into many films, and is such a powerful tale that it's credited with helping to define our contemporary understanding of Christmas.

But a fresh look at this all-time classic, reminds us that it's far more than just a feel-good festive tale featuring a miserly old humbug. In fact, the story of Ebenezer Scrooge and his tormenting spirits helps us to consider what is of eternal value today.

Dickens set out to persuade his readers to summon the spirit of Christmas not just at Christmas, but also for all the year. His message has a timeless, universal quality, like all the best works of art.

The book's main character is the mean and intimidating Ebenezer Scrooge, who lives to make money and very little else. He certainly has no use for religion or sentimentality.

One Christmas Eve, however, Scrooge receives a terrifying wake-up call. The spirit of his business partner, Jacob Marley, who died seven Christmas Eves previous, comes to visit, bound and wrapped in heavy chains. Marley has been condemned to roam the face of the earth, tormented in death by the things he neglected to value in life.

He is desperate to give his old colleague a final chance to avoid the same fate. 'My spirit never walked beyond our counting-house,' he warns Scrooge. 'My spirit never roved beyond the narrow limits of our money-changing hole . . .' This, he makes clear, is

Scrooge's last opportunity to turn from his selfish and insular ways. Marley's spirit instructs him to wait for three more spirits of Christmas past, present and future. Reluctantly, Scrooge understands that this is for real, as he sees Marley float away to join a crowd of tormented souls who are wailing and moaning in the night sky.

On the stroke of one o'clock, the Spirit of Christmas Past arrives, and takes him on an unforgettable trip down memory lane, on a visit to his own childhood.

Scrooge is astonished to see old, familiar faces playing happily in the open air. As the Spirit takes him into a schoolroom, however, they see a lonely little boy sitting by the fire, whose only companion is the book he is reading.

Scrooge remembers his loneliness, and how he longed for the presence and warmth of friends. He recalls his past desires for the love and approval of his family, but then sees all the people who tried to reach out to him, who attempted to stop his slide into self-absorption and an increasing preoccupation with personal security.

He sees his former fiancée, Belle, who came a poor second to Scrooge's passion for wealth. 'A golden idol displaces me,' she complains to him from the past. 'All hopes have merged to a master passion; the thought of money engrosses you!'

Dickens explores, through Scrooge's terrifying ordeal, the love of money compared with the value of relationships. Scrooge's whole life has come to revolve around his counting-house. His insatiable appetite consumes him for more. To him, Christmas has become nothing more than a 'time for finding yourself a year older, but not an hour richer'.

Today, in the 21st century, we can fall into a similar trap, seeing money – and the things it can buy – as the answer to our problems, especially if our lives have not been that happy, like the young Ebenezer Scrooge's. We perceive the 'good life' as being about an abundance of bigger, brighter and better things.

Jacob Marley's ghostly visit is not just a wake-up call for Scrooge. As we hear his words, we should make sure we haven't lost out on the things that money can't buy. We all need money, of course, but it's possible to pay too high a price for it. It's as if society has caught a cultural disease called 'affluenza'. The symptoms include always wanting more, despite what we already have. And then there's the insatiable desire for 'success' without experiencing contentment. Consistently, we choose our career over family. And we seem unwilling to settle for less than the best of everything.

The Second spirit

If Scrooge has been shaken by the visit of the first spirit, then the second is no less disturbing. The Spirit of Christmas Present arrives to take Scrooge on a tour of the people he now knows. He finds himself standing in the home of his poor clerk, Bob Cratchit, where he feels the warmth of a large and friendly family who are making the best of what little they can afford on the tiny salary Scrooge pays. He experiences their anxiety over the fate of Tiny Tim, the Cratchit's sick, youngest child.

Scrooge is clearly shown the effects of his selfish nature; but the Spirit helps him understand that even though he is utterly hard-hearted, others have not entirely given up on him. As they sit down to their feeble Christmas dinner, Bob Cratchit thinks to toast his employer, despite protests from his wife.

The Spirit of Christmas Present then shows Scrooge the harsh reality of life on the streets, together with the absolute determination of the families who live there to stay out of the prisons

and workhouses, whatever the cost. Scrooge has never before seen the need to help anyone other than himself. He's always believed that the poor should go to the institutions provided – 'If they would rather die, they had better do it, and decrease the surplus population.'

Then, the Spirit reveals two hauntingly thin and deathly children from within his cloak. They are called IGNORANCE and WANT – two of the grim realities of Victorian life. The Spirit describes them as the 'children of all who walk the earth unseen'. On their brow is written 'DOOM'.

But it is not the quivering, hollow children who are doomed. As Scrooge pleads for them to be removed from his sight, the Spirit explains that ignorance and want 'spells the downfall of you and all those who deny their existence'.

Before you put someone in his or her place, you should put yourself in his or hers. How much poverty do we allow ourselves to see? The Spirit responds, 'They are hidden, but they live.' Dickens holds a mirror not just to Scrooge's face, but also to ours. How do we treat the poor, the weak and the vulnerable? Do we shield ourselves from the needs of the poor and downtrodden?

After all, we are not on this earth to see through one another, but to see one another through.

The Final Spirit

Then comes the final spirit, the Spirit of Christmas Future, who has no face and does not speak. It merely points. Scrooge looks to where the Spirit is leading him, and sees the Cratchit family again, worn down in their struggle against poverty, and now without Tiny Tim, who has died for lack of proper medical care.

The Spirit takes Scrooge to visit the house of a man who has died in his sleep. A maid and a cleaner are dividing up his belongings before the undertaker arrives. Two associates are discussing whether it's even necessary to hold a funeral service, since no one would bother to come.

'But who is this man?' asks Scrooge. The Spirit leads him to a grave, whose headstone bears the name 'Ebenezer Scrooge'. It's a chilling reminder that no one lives forever; that the journey of life is brief. As the Bible says, 'our days on earth are like a shadow' (1 Chronicles 29:15, NIV).

This is the life-changing moment when Scrooge understands that it's now or never. He asks whether it's possible to mend his ways and so alter his life and destiny. Surely the Spirits wouldn't be visiting him if not? As Christmas morning dawns and he wakes, once more, to the world, Scrooge realises that he has been given a reprieve. He has another chance to be more human – just as Dickens believed we have all been given another opportunity, because of the birth of Jesus Christ.

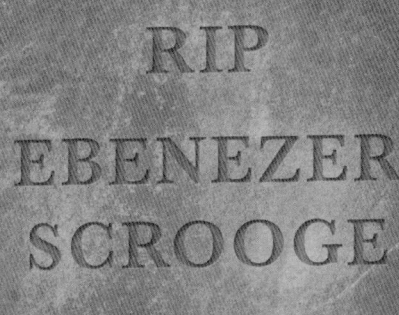

Many of us will recognise the struggles of Ebenezer Scrooge in our own lives. Many of us have been hurt as we grew up. Many of us pass up the offer of friendship or kindness out of a fear of rejection. Scrooge was a man who lived in a prison of his own making, the doors shut and sealed with a bitterness which he would not let go.

In fact, Dickens symbolises the consequence of our selfish actions by the chain that traps Jacob Marley's spirit and weighs him down. Marley tells Scrooge that he alone forged it in life: 'I made it link by link, and yard by yard.'

His chains were forged with regrets, which he could not release, and hurts he would not forgive. And as he stands before Scrooge, he can see the even greater chains that bind his old colleague: 'Would you know the weight and length of the strong coil you bear yourself?' asks Marley. 'It was full as heavy and as long as this, seven Christmas Eves ago. You have laboured on it since. It is a ponderous chain!'

The good news is that we can learn from the past, to change now so that we can create a better future. Just as the Spirits of Christmas wanted Scrooge to change for good, so God knows us better than we know ourselves, and loves us enough to help us to change and make a difference.

Christmas is the time and place where God draws back the curtain so we can see his face. Jesus has come to free us, because we are bound by chains. In fact, because of Jesus, we can commemorate the past, consecrate the present and contemplate the future. Jesus came to give us a new outlook on life.

The good news is that we, like Scrooge, are still alive. It's not too late: we can choose to change. Life can only be understood backwards, but it must be lived forwards. Whatever our past has been, we can have a better future.

At the heart of *A Christmas Carol* lies Scrooge's transformation. From a selfish, greedy and bitter old man, we see him become a grateful, generous and compassionate figure. A man filled with deep regret sees his life transformed, to the point where Dickens concludes 'he became as good a friend, as good a master, and as good a man, as the good old city knew'.

Things do not change. We do. Scrooge learns his lesson, and experiences what amounts to a 'conversion'. He responds by changing his ways and living out the lessons that he learnt on

that Christmas Eve. He repents and changes his destiny.

Jesus, the Son of God, invites us to do the same. What better time than Christmas to receive forgiveness, renew our faith, release our fears and rebuild our friendships?

In case you are still making a Christmas list, here are some timeless gifts that won't cost you anything except, perhaps, a little pride. You could mend a quarrel, release a grudge, lessen your demands on others, apologise, forgive someone who has treated you wrongly, find a forgotten friend, write an overdue thank-you note, point out one thing you appreciate most about someone you live with or work with, tell someone you love them, or give something away.

You cannot do a kindness too soon, because you never know how soon it will be too late.

We talk about 'the birth of new ideas' and of hope being 'born' in the human heart. Why not let Jesus be born into your life, this Christmas time? It takes a conscious, personal decision to become a follower of Jesus, which begins by acknowledging that we all need him – to forgive us for what we have done wrong, and to guide us into *real* life, the life he promised to give us 'to the full' by his Holy Spirit and experience a dynamic, living relationship with God our creator – is surely worth it.

If you want to make this Christmas one to remember, then there's no need to wait any longer. If you ask Jesus to forgive your past, and invite him to enter your Christmas present, then your life will be transformed – now, and for good.

Dickens sent a message to us in the form of an amazing story. God sends his message in the form of his Son, Jesus Christ, who lives today. In the words of the wonderful carol 'O Little Town of Bethlehem', we can invite Jesus to be with us, like he was, all those years ago at the first Christmas:

O holy Child of Bethlehem, descend to us, we pray;

Cast out our sin, and enter in, be born in us today.

We hear the Christmas angels the great glad tidings tell;

O come to us, abide with us, our Lord Emmanuel!

May God grant you the light of Christmas, which is faith;

The warmth of Christmas, which is love;

The radiance of Christmas, which is purity;

The righteousness of Christmas, which is justice;

The belief in Christmas, which is truth;

The all of Christmas, which is Christ.

As we celebrate the birth of Jesus, may God grant you all these things – not just at Christmas, but also throughout the New Year and all the years to come.